T.

Thanks

For Gift

The Courage
to Conquer Fear

of Music
you are a
blessing

(260) 804-0301
Guice Gregory @ Yahoo.
com

Jill

The Courage to Conquer Fear

The Seven Spiritual Keys

Rev. Gregory C. Guice

To order additional copies of this book, contact:
Xlibris Corporation
1-888-795-4274
www.Xlibris.com
Orders@Xlibris.com
64861

CONTENTS

In dedication:

First, let me begin my expression of gratitude to God for all things.

This book is dedicated to the memory of my mother and father, Corrine Collins and Rufus Guice. A special expression of love is given to the presence and memory of my daughter Morgan Imani Guice. Her divine transition has given me the motivation and inspiration to bring these pages to life; for those who knew her spirit would tell you how much courage and love she displayed in her life.

These pages are also dedicated to my beloved wife and family, Francine Guice, Johnny Collins, Roderic Collins, Rochelle Guice, Deborah Guice, the Bowens family, William Hytower, and to all my extended family members for we know that family is love. Thank you for the belief and love that you have constantly given to me.

To my daughter and granddaughter that I love with no end and to Dr. Merrin I. Guice and Sydney Mitchell, for in you I know only love.

To Christina and Jacquelyn Segars always remember to strive for your highest good.

I also want to take this opportunity to express my gratitude to my Unity Church Community, family and friends from Unity Village to Fort Wayne, from Detroit to Lake Orion, and from Jamaica to Bermuda—thank you—for you have given to me the encouragement and knowledge to say yes to write this book.

To my Nigerian spiritual community whose continuous out pouring of love embraced me with the awareness of my heritage, I want to say thank you.

My life is filled with gratitude and appreciation for so many inspiring individuals whose light and truth brought inspiration into my world.

Thank you Deb Derderian for the hard work and commitment you provide me by reviewing this material.

Thank you Judy and Dianne for your valuable contributions to this material.

Finally this book is dedicated to anyone who has ever felt the paralyzing grip of fear and reached out to that higher presence; asking for the strength to overcome.

Introduction . . .

"THE LORD IS MY LIGHT AND MY SALVATION WHOM SHALL I FEAR"

Sometimes a message is given to each of us as a unique revelation or insight from God and it opens our mind in special ways. I had such a message when speaking to a group of young men about things that motivated and inspired them.

As a teacher and pastor, I speak frequently to many different groups of people on all kinds of topics. But recently, I was speaking to a group of young men at a community center that provided mentoring and tutoring support and they talked about their personal heroes, those who inspired them with determination and courage.

Some named people like Labron James, Kobe Bryant and other sports or entertainment celebrities. Others touched on their big brothers, teachers and friends who inspired them to reach higher for what they wanted in life. Then there were those special few who shared how their parents had given them words of encouragement.

In that same conversation, I asked them what they feared about their future. What, for them, brings fear, worry and doubt into their lives? One young man talked about how scared he was to go to school, walking in areas where drug dealers lined the streets of his neighborhood. And I remembered all too well feeling the exact same way as a kid in my neighborhood. Another young man feared that he would end up in jail or dead like so many of his friends, and closer to home, his own brother.

Then one young man asked a question, "Why do people have to live in a neighborhood where everyone's afraid to walk in their own streets at night and sometimes in the day. I am afraid for my grandmother; she's too old and doesn't have anyone to help her".

Hearing their stories, listening to their questions, seeing fear and anger on their faces brought back many overwhelming memories for me. I was able see myself in their eyes and I recalled that same song of sadness and despair that I had felt as a child, captured with words and images of our shared reality of fear.

According to The American Heritage Dictionary fear is: "an emotion of alarm and agitation cause by the expectation or realization of danger" or terror which becomes an overpowering energy that creates panic that effects our entire state of mind. As I listened to their stories of death, crime and poverty, it made me deeply aware that our children are living in a world and society where we embrace and accept *fear* as a daily reality. The stories and questions from these young men became the catalyst that sparked a fire of inspiration that burned within me.

Have we given to our children a "spirit of fear" that shackles them from moving forward with their lives? If so, it is as false a reality as a demon at night hiding in the closet. Do their stories point to a world that lacks the courage or will power to meet the challenges of fear or more importantly, the courage and faith to believe in the strength and character to face our adversities and tribulations? Have we created a world that continually plants seeds of fear into our consciousness?

As I listened to those young men, I began to realize that we must rediscover and reclaim the courage within ourselves to conquer fear. I am not writing this just for the youth of our society. I am writing this book to open all hearts and minds to see the deep concern and need to bring this discussion forward and address the fear that plagues our society.

There is also a personal reason that encourages me to take this stand for our young men and women who feel fear growing up. Their story is also my story. Growing up on the tough streets of Detroit, Michigan, I needed someone to say to me, "have no fears" or to give me direction to overcome my fears.

I searched for ways to free myself from this demon fear that I knew for years and that preyed on my consciousness. It lingered within me as I walked through the streets of Detroit as a boy and I can see it in the eyes of our youth whether they are living on those same streets in downtown Detroit or in the suburbs across our nation.

Today we are witnessing and experiencing a foundational change in the world as we take steps into the 21 century. For many, it hasn't felt so good. Change, especially such radical change that we have experienced this first new millennium decade, has come fast and furious.

Some call this new millennium the "Age of Aquarius", which is predicted to offer much in the form of communication, technology, spirituality and science to meet man's need to expand within our world and grow as a society.

This new beginning has come into our world like a comet in the night bringing with it not only the wonderful gifts of scientific and technological breakthroughs, but challenges that threaten our society and ripple across all continents of the world.

The task at hand is critical and one does not need to be a prophet to see the challenges facing our society and our families: poverty, homelessness, education, crime, the continued threat of war, hunger and global governance. Each of these large social and personal issues can lace minds with fear, worry and doubt. This fear prevents us from connecting to our oneness with God and that can lead us into a hopeless path of victimization and destruction.

I believe, and I have experienced, that the response to the challenge of this new century will be our ability to demonstrate the presence of God within. Connecting to our God-presence will inspire us, strengthen us, guide us and give us the courage needed today and tomorrow to determine our legacy.

Along with the challenges that face us as adults are the fears and anxieties of our children, those same young men and women from all walks of life who will be the recipients of our decisions and efforts and who will reap the benefits of our consciousness and actions.

This book is designed to inspire, inform, and provide a way to reclaim our courage and the will power to meet the challenges we face. My goal in writing this book is to share the foundational spiritual knowledge that has been demonstrated over the years by the teachings of those enlightened souls and way-showers who taught us how to overcome the challenges before us and within us, from Joshua to Jesus. But more than anything else, my desire is to give hope to our children to know that they have within themselves the courage to conquer the things they fear.

Through the stories shared within these pages of famous people and everyday individuals, we will take a journey that will deepen our understanding of how fear impacts our lives and the understanding and courage it takes to overcome this inner demon called fear.

This new beginning, this new era, will require the courage and spirit of Joshua, a biblical character whose fearlessness allowed him to see beyond the challenges and the doubts of his peers. It will take a courage that will be inspiring and motivational to all those who bear witness to this movement and presence of Christ.

"Our deepest fear is not that we are inadequate. Our deepest fear is that we are powerful beyond measure. It is our light not our darkness that frightens us. We ask ourselves who am I to be brilliant, gorgeous, talented and fabulous? Actually who are you not to be? You are a child of God. Your playing small doesn't serve the world. There's nothing enlightened about shrinking so that other people won't feel insecure around you. We were born to make manifest the glory of God that is within us. It is not just in some of us; it's in everyone. And as we let our light shine, we unconsciously give other people permission to do the same. As we are liberated from our fear, our presence automatically liberates others."

(Marianne Williamson)

Chapter One

FACING OUR FEARS

"SEARCH FOR THE SEED OF GOOD IN EVERY ADVERSITY."

(OG MANDINO)

In our society there are thousands of individuals who are seeking medication and treatment for fear. Their level of anxiety is causing them to lose grip on their personal well being. They see life from a defeatist perspective and wear this belief as a badge of victimization.

For them, fear has become a demon that grows as anxiety increases with every news broadcast of a world gone mad or telecast that features the raging increase of crime in our communities or our failing economy. The parade of journalist's commentary that paint a picture of death, destruction, war and corruption has fed this beast that lives within our minds and feeds our thirst for more.

What so many individuals don't understand is that *fear* can act like a narcotic. We may know fear and its destructive ability, but we soon find that its true measure is an addictive quality that quietly grows stronger within us if we accept it as our reality. It can begin as simply as listening to the bad news of the day. Then, something inside our minds latches on and we begin to ponder and meditate about the news. We call our family and friends to talk about it, pumping up the fear level and spreading more of the dis-ease around. Fear becomes the reality show we tune into to see each night for hours of news and commentary.

Fear, according to the founder of the Unity Movement, Charles Fillmore, is described as "one of the most subtle and destructive errors that the carnal mind in man experiences. Fear is a paralysis of mental action; it weakens both mind and body. Not only does it weaken the mind and the body, it affects the structure of government and how people respond to each other. When a society is crippled by fear, it stops the circulation and growth of a community and reacts in a victim thought process that sees only defeat and puts out a communication of worry, doubt, and unworthiness.

These words of Charles Fillmore and other Unity, New Thought, and Christian Spiritual writers helped me to see this massive challenge that we face; a challenge that I quickly learned is a spiritual reflection of our belief system. We hold the key to this awareness and to this emotional challenge called fear. Jesus, the greatest of all teachers, the highest embodiment of Christ, understood that in His ministry, God is Love and in that love there is no fear.

If we learn to face this spiritual challenge of fear early in our life, it can impact our lives in many ways and through many experiences. I will never forget the fear I felt as a young man of seventeen working for my older brother who was at the time, responsible for the delivering the local newspaper to a community high rise housing project. For those of you who may have never lived in that setting, it an environment that's filled with people from all segments of life.

One day, as I helped him deliver the papers to the residents of one of these buildings, I noticed a man in the hallway, rubbing his arms, looking nervous and in distress. To me he looked like a drug addict. Fearful, I quickly walked toward an old, unstable elevator. As I hurried, I noticed him out of the corner of my eye walking fast behind me. Just as the door was closing, he jumped in next to me. My heart was racing, pounding like a drum. Without a word, he pulled out a cold black pistol and in one motion pointed it in my face. I was paralyzed with fear as the held the gun next to my cheek and said, "Give me all your money if you want to live."

I felt drained and numb. My mind went blank and I struggled for a single breath or a single thought. Then, I heard a quiet small voice within me echoing a prayer that my mother always said to me:

"The lord is my shepherd; I shall not want. He maketh me to lie down in green pastures; He leadeth me beside the still waters. He restoreth my soul: he leadeth me in the path of righteousness for his name sake. Yea though I walk through the valley of the shadow of death, I will fear no evil;"

I held fast to that prayer, repeating it again and again in my mind. Then suddenly, for no reason, the junkie looked at me and said "get the hell out of here". I ran away as fast as I could.

On that day, I learned a lesson about this emotion called fear; that it can come at any moment. It can make you feel helpless, at the mercy of others or events. But I also learned that there is a presence within that will rise up to meet fear at the crossroads of our consciousness and surround us with assurance, blessed assurance. This voice of assurance, I believe, is always present within each of us.

Sometimes it is hard to hear it for ourselves when the din of bad news and anxiety rattle our minds. As you listen to the heart beat of a community, you can hear the fear of the people echo in barber shops and at shopping malls. You can hear their pain and despair as the reaction to the bad news the media and government continue to broadcast about the social and economic dangers of today.

I heard such a man voice his fatigue and frustration at the endless bombardment of doomsday thoughts while getting my hair trimmed at the local barber shop recently. This gentleman paced the floor in a frantic motion repeating, the question "What am I going do? I'm tired, I'm tired". You could feel his pain and you could hear his fear. The barber shop became quiet as if each of us had been drawn into his desperate world of anxiety and hopelessness. He had lost his job and began to blame everyone from the government to his wife who left him some years ago for his troubles.

Finally, one of the barbers, noted for his wisdom, tried to console him by telling him that all is not lost and above everything else, "brother, don't give up now". Those words caused him to stop pacing the floor. He looked at the author of those words and asked him what should he do? "Don't give up!" the barber repeated, this time with energy and passion.

The next few moments we all became philosophers and psychologists as we examined ourselves and society. Even though we traveled light years with our conversation, we discovered that there was one constant element that we agreed upon; the impact of fear on our lives. We discussed how fear creates a defeated mentality, a victim's attitude, which fosters a non-competitive drive in the soul, pushing all of us to believe that life is a reflection of limitations instead of unlimited resources and possibilities.

Each of us at that barber shop shared our brother's plight. He became a symbol for what was taking place in our community of lost souls; people mentally and spiritually searching for help as they discussed the fears which engulfed them. After this a gentleman left the barber shop and just as he was closing the doors, to no one's surprise, within a few minutes, there followed behind him another brother asking for help and hope.

Chapter Two

THE CHALLENGE BEGINS WITHIN

"Courage comes by taking action before you are forced to."

(Iyanla Vanzant)

There are millions of stories that reflect this demon we call "F-E-A-R". It has been summarized as, "False Evidence Appearing Real". I see it as, "**F**AITHLESS **E**MOTIONS **A**CTING **R**EAL.

I have found that a key component in our arsenal to combat fear is *FAITH*. When we face our fear or anxiety, it is our *faith* that gives us the courage to deal with these challenges. When fear enters our consciousness and begins to affect our belief system, we lose our faith and we begin to see from the eyes of worry, doubt, and confusion and a host of other faithless emotions acting real.

The gospel duet of "Mary Mary" has a song whose words spoke of this faith and inner spirit titled "Can't give Up Now". The first few lines of their lyrics are:

"There will be mountain that I will have to climb,
And there will be battles that I will have to fight.
But victory or defeat, it's up to me to decide,
But how can I expect to win if I never try
I just can't give up now

I've come too far from where I started from
Nobody told me the road would be easy
And I don't believe he brought me this far to leave me now . . ."

Many such songs and spiritual stories can shape our imagination and help build a foundation for choosing *faith* over *fear*. Songs and stories of spiritual courage and strength demonstrate an inner presence within mankind that has been able to conquer fear through love and faith throughout time.

As a youth, it was mandatory that church have an equal part in my education. I was taught biblical stories that stimulated my belief system and expressed universal truths of overcoming. These stories brought me an inner awareness that, 'with God, whom shall I fear; for I know that all things are possible'.

An example of this type of story took place in early biblical history. It is the story of Joshua and Caleb. As the Bible story goes, Moses selected 12 men, one from each of the twelve tribe of Israel. Their mission was to spy on the land of Canaan, the land God promised to the Israelites. When these twelve spies slipped into Canaan, they found men that looked like giants and a group mentality of fear and defeat took over. How could they conquer these frightful people? How could they fight these giants living in their land of God's promise?

When they returned home and questions were asked about the land of Canaan, ten of the twelve immediately stated their fears that the giants who resided in this land were too fierce and could not be conquered. They encouraged Moses and Aaron to surrender the idea of ever living in Canaan. However, two of the twelve, Joshua and Caleb, stood fast in their faith and belief in God's promise and said without a doubt, these people could be conquered and they could win their new home land.

The ten shared their voices of fear to Moses, expressed as faithless emotions when compared to Joshua and Caleb who had no hesitation moving forward. Joshua and Caleb's determination and faith in God's guarantee would not allow the appearance or the thought of anything less than the ability to successfully move toward God's promise of this land for the children of Israel.

How did it turn out? Moses did not believe the naysayers. He listened to the inspiring voices of Joshua and Caleb and did not allow the fear or the appearance of giants to take away his dream. He never lived to see his Promised Land. Joshua and Caleb, however, never lost their faith and later in life, led his people victoriously into their land of milk and honey.

What a great example of faith conquering fear. Their story is our story today, for so many of us are in a place in this world where we're seeking a new beginning or searching for a place called hope. The lost job, the home foreclosure, the poverty, the change, the financial crisis we face today in our lives are appearing like the giants that inhabit the land of Canaan. These various issues are situations that seem insurmountable. They seem to overwhelm our reality.

So somewhere in our consciousness, we must make a choice to either become aligned to fear or to faith around these issues. We can chose to accept the attitude like the spies who witnessed only fear and inadequacy or we can choose to take on the attitude of Joshua or Caleb who would not see defeat, but who upheld the attitude that understands that with God we can do all things.

The truth is that we can make a choice to incorporate a spirit of Joshua, to let go of fear and replace it with faith. Joshua's name in the bible means "Jah is savior", "Jehovah is deliverer". The Hebrew name is identical with the name Jesus whose foundation is "I AM THAT I AM". This is the consciousness of Joshua, a consciousness that identifies with an inner presence of Christ, that understands the power of I AM.

This awareness is the central key to facing the challenges in our life, large or small. The awareness is to know that our ability to see **our** Promised Land is built within each and every person in proportion to their **faith**.

Developing this conscious recognition and understanding that *faith* is the cornerstone for our spiritual foundation allows us to gather our courage and move forward. The Joshua spirit is a plane of consciousness that has a spiritual

understanding and knows that inner strength given by the presence and power of I AM, the foundation of Christ within us. This awareness allows us to be fueled by an inner faith which knows that with Christ, we can do all things.

We have to be conscious not to build our spiritual foundation on fear, for fear will attach itself to our belief system and become a parasite that limits our expectation and, like the other spies sent into Canaan, we will quickly begin to see giants within our minds. As it was stated with Job in the bible, "the things I fear come upon me".

I have a friend who inspired me to think about the story of Joshua and Caleb. Paul's life spiraled downhill and he became trapped in the elements of the streets. Drugs and crime were stepping stones for him. Finally, his life of crime and abuse landed him in prison. Determined to start his life again when he got out, he struggled with the fear of what work he would do to survive. Like so many returning ex-cons, he couldn't find employment. He soon became homeless and gripped by fear. But somewhere in the mist of his despair and desperation, he reached out to God in prayer, asking for guidance and help. He told me that it was during that time of deepest his fear, an idea came to him.

He borrowed a few dollars from friends added the few dollars he had been able to save and invested it all in a large bag of shelled peanuts. He found a corner in his neighborhood where there was a continuous flow of traffic and packaged up his peanuts into small quantities. He dressed every day in shirt and tie as he stood on his corner "office" to work selling bags of peanuts. Eventually, he was inspired to add bottles of water as a part of his product line. From that time on, his life was no longer the same because *he* was no longer the same.

In the beginning, it was hard work. His constant prayers and steadfast faith kept away the demons of fear. He was able to grow his business little by little and get by. In a few short years he became known as the Peanut Man. He eventually expanded his business and was able to hire other individuals. He built his business into a legacy for others to see that when you let go of fear, you will discover within you the courage to move forward.

"If you want to conquer fear, do not sit home and think about it. Go out and get busy." (Dale Carnegie)

From the inception of his divine idea, he never saw himself unemployed or lost. As he focused his mind on God, his newly found, unyielding faith, replaced his fear. Through his Joshua spirit, my friend was able to realize that the courage to challenge his fears rests within him. There, in that sacred space, he found his promise land.

Chapter Three

WHEN CHALLENGING FEAR WITH COURAGE: IT CAN CHANGE THE WORLD

"HE GIVES STRENGTH TO THE WEARY AND INCREASE THE POWER OF THE WEAK.
. . . BUT THOSE WHO WAIT ON THE LORD SHALL RENEW THEIR STRENGTH.
THEY WILL SOAR ON WINGS LIKE EAGLES;
THEY WILL NOT RUN AND GROW WEARY; THEY WILL WALK AND NOT BE FAINT."

(ISAIAH 40: 29, 31)

Within our own communities and families we can discover a wealth of inspirational stories of the human soul challenging the demons of fear. There are stories both from the biblical and personal pages of life that are carved and etched with pens of courage that help to rewrite the path of humanity.

Biblically, we shared the story of Joshua and Caleb, whose insightfulness and courage made them some of the many heroes within the Bible's holy book. Another such story of inspiration is the life of Joseph who was sold into slavery in Egypt by his brothers. His story is one of overcoming an intended plight of darkness, a story that demonstrates how that presence of God will alter another's desired path for you.

Joseph's brothers out of jealousy and envy, intended to harm and enslavement him and they even made it appear to their father that he was dead. But Joseph did not let fear become rooted into his consciousness. He did not let his enslavement block his ability to see God's goodness unfolding all around him.

Through a series of events that seemed both blessed and cursed, he kept his faith and went from being sold into slavery to ruling the land of Egypt. His ability to listen to divine mind and to see with the gift of imagination allowed him to rise above the fear and bad intentions of others. He was able to follow his inner divine guidance and prepare the Egyptians for an upcoming famine that would last for seven years. He saved not only the Egyptians but his own family including his brothers. God's intention for Joseph was good regardless of what his brothers may have sought to create.

Joseph's name represents the faculty of "Imagination", and when we let fear enter into our state of being, it blocks our imaginative process. We then fail to see the unlimited possibilities that can exist around us. When we use our imagination, we allow the presence of the Holy Spirit to open our inner eye to see beyond limitation and darkness, to clothe our mind with new ideas.

Today, Joseph's story can be viewed metaphysically to illustrate how so many of us are feeling trapped into a slave mentally. Our "peace of mind" has been sold into slavery, bonded by the continue threats of limitation and lack in our community. The demigod **fear** has created chains of oppression that have crippled our imagination to see beyond a famine of unemployment, and poverty, crime and abuse.

Yet, when we enter into the state of consciousness as Joseph did, we can attain mastery using our imaginative faculty and overcome our fear-based emotions. We then break the chains of oppression that holds our mind in a paralyzing grip. In scripture it states, "We are more than conquerors through him that loved us".

I believe we are truly blessed to have a man of courage similar to Joseph, who is serving as President of United States speaking to our society and stating that we must have *"Hope over Fear"*. He demonstrates continuously the spirit of Joshua and Joseph to uplift him to see our promised land can be achieved, that famine will end and we will have plenty once again.

President Barack Obama's gift to us is one that calls out to our soul and expresses encouraging and inspiring words to the world that we must have a spirit of courage during this difficult time. He stresses that we must be willing to work together, to have the audacity to believe in each other.

He states, *"The journey will be difficult. The road will be long. I face this challenge with profound humility and knowledge of my own limitations. But I also face it with limitless faith in the capacity of the American people."*

When we capture this same spirit as President Obama and those light workers of this epic time, we will not let fear, nor worry enslave us into a consciousness of bondage for we will know and declare these words in the mist of despair or a challenge . . . **"YES WE CAN", "YES WE CAN"**.

Across this world there are other stories of individuals who dare to challenge this faithless energy of fear. These individuals rally the courage of the human soul to do the impossible. The story of Immaculee Ilibagiza is a testimony of both fear and courage. She expressed to the world how she survived the Rwanda genocide in 1994 along with seven other women. She shared how they lived in a cramped bathroom hiding in a local pastor's house for 91 days and how she had to witness first hand, the brutal murder of her family members.

Throughout this ordeal, Immaculee was able to retain her voracious faith and connection to that inner presence of God. She believed that this inner spirit which lived within her, gave her the hope and strength to survive.

We may never know the fear that she felt during those unbelievable times, or the horror that lived at her doorstep, day in and day out never knowing if this day would be her last day. The greatest lesson she gave us through her suffering was a lesson of forgiveness and unconditional love to her country and to humanity.

When the sacredness of love is stronger than fear, fear loses its grip on our mental state of being, and our faith combined with love becomes strengthened. That sacred love is the ingredient that makes the Immaculee Ilibagiza story so remarkable. She overcame her fear, she withstood the emotional surge that flowed within her like a sea of terror, and she held on to an unyielding faith that God will deliver her from evil.

"You can gain strength, courage and confidence by every experience in which you really stop to look fear in the face. You are able to say to yourself, 'I've lived through this horror. I can take the next thing that comes along.' You must do the thing you think you cannot do." (Eleanor Roosevelt)

Those individuals whose courage overcame their challenges of fear are examples of the human spirit that is filled with the resilience of our history. Their stories are the fuel that we share and benefit from together as we encounter our personal challenges.

"FOR GOD HAS NOT GIVEN US A SPIRIT OF FEAR, BUT OF POWER AND LOVE AND OF A SOUND MIND." (2Ti 1:7)

Chapter Four

RECLAIMING OUR COMMUNITIES FROM FEAR

"I FEEL THAT THE MOST IMPORTANT REQUIREMENT IN SUCCESS IS LEARNING TO OVERCOME FAILURE. YOU MUST LEARN TO TOLERATE IT, BUT NEVER ACCEPT IT."

(REGGIE JACKSON)

There is another aspect of Fear that we must bring into our discussion, and that is the critical impact that FEAR is having on our collective communities, our youth, and on the world as a whole. We have been looking at how this fear can paralyze us individually, but the damage that it can create within a community, within our society, within our children which can take years or generations to remove.

We can see the effects of this systematic virus of fear as it begins to ripple throughout our modern society. The challenge for us, as it has always been throughout history, is that once our communities become infected by this faithless emotion it spreads through the collective body until some counter-agent of perfect love becomes the healing energy that reduces the parasitical influences.

It's like the warmth that a mother gives to her children who are filled with the fear of the night, the unknown, the boogie man. She embraces them with the insurance of unconditional love surrounding them with the knowingness that she will never desert them, nor let harm come to them.

We don't have to look too far beyond our very own families to find courageous individuals as examples of light and inspiration. They are there before us each and every day. For instance, teachers defy common logic by tackling the bleak picture of many children who don't seem to care about life. These teachers transform their fears into their love of teaching and learning to give their students a chance to reach beyond their physical environments or the social limitations of their birth. These instructors embrace an attitude for their students and that says "Yes I Can".

There are also the 'Kool Aid' moms and the block club presidents in our communities who still believe that their neighborhoods don't have to become the playground for gangsters and thugs. These many courageous individuals will never be written about in history books or given city awards or parades. They simply go about their business standing up to the fears of our community, defying the thought of the appearance of hopelessness.

These spiritual leaders, our friends and neighbors, who carry the spirit of Joshua, are the light workers that serve as an example of how perfect love can erase fear. They are our ministers and other caring souls in our community who see the neighborhood not limited to the appearance of poverty or wealth, but who see the value of the children within the community. They put their love into action as they invest words of faith and demonstrate strength and courage to the families and children of our communities.

These individuals are the heroes who believe that God has not given us a spirit of fear.

We are in a time of world history where humanity is calling forth spiritually minded men and women who are willing to stand against this challenge called fear. Like a disease that affects the body, the mind, and the soul, it quietly and at times explosively enters into our system, remaining there till we pour perfect love into the wounds of our consciousness.

Dr. Martin Luther King Jr. internalized this calling, this inner courage to change our world as he stood at the doorway of time filled with perfect love and faith. He stood in his belief that America must change from a land of hatred and fear. He knew that there was a presence within him that would not yield to fear. He knew this demon fear feasted on the spiritually weak. Dr. King's courage was built on LOVE, and as the civil rights campaign marched throughout the south, with death threats and angry hate filled mobs, he encouraged all to stand against injustice by demonstrating peaceful defiance.

Dr. King knew the perfect ingredient to overcome this plague of fear that was gripping our country, and he knew that the battle could only be won with non-violence and love.

"When our days become dreary with low hovering clouds of despair, and when our nights become darker than midnight, let us remember that there is a creative force in this universe, working to pull down the gigantic mountains of evils, a power that is able to make a way out of no way and transform dark yesterdays into bright tomorrows. Let us realize the arc of the moral universe is long but it bends toward justice."

Today our children, our community, our inner self, are calling us to retake our consciousness back from fear, to reconnect with that God presence within ourselves through prayer and meditation. We can also choose as Dr. King to reclaim "peace of mind", hope for humanity, and to march with the motivation to build a world that responds to love and not fear, or hate.

We must relearn that our healing begins when we awaken our souls to the Truth of its being and become conscious of the One Presence and One Power that lives within us as infinite good. When we begin to redefine this conscious alignment, denying that fear has any power over us, we can then erase this false and negative belief and march in the glory of a new beginning echoing the teaching of Jesus Christ, Mahatma Gandhi, and those souls who dared to see Hope over Fear.

"You shall know the Truth and the Truth shall set you free" (John 8:32)

As we begin to make this shift individually, we begin a process that will alter the consciousness of our planet collectively: in our communities, for our brothers and sisters and even the very cells of our own being will become charged with this reawakened thought, this power of I AM.

"Within you is a limitless, unborn potential of creativity and substance, and the present experience can be your great opportunity to give birth to it. Thus, if you will, the tragedy can become a blessing, the disadvantage can become an advantage, the failure can become an opportunity, and the disappointment can become "His" appointment . . ." (Eric Butterworth)

Chapter Five

"PEACE BE STILL"

"The winds and the waves shall obey my will
Peace be still,
Whether the wrath of the storm-tossed sea
or demons,
Or man, or whatever be.
No water can swallow the ship where lies
The Master of ocean and earth and skies;
They shall sweetly obey my will,
Peace Be Still, Peace Be Still,
They all shall sweetly obey my will;

The words of the song by James Cleveland were keys to my mother's inner sanctuary where she entered to reclaim her truth, that fear had no power over her. This attitude became the gift that she extended to all of her children, an attitude that resonated within us as a spirit of overcoming.

My mother was a strong mentor to me. Whenever the storms of life came surging in and their waves pounded on her mind, she simply would become still and go to that sacred space within and in that moment she would sway from side to side as she hummed the James Cleveland song, "Peace Be Still". I would watch her enter into that sacred place that only God and my mother knew. I can still hear the words of that song running through my mind, opening my heart to the beauty and healing energy they gave me.

I am grateful for her courage and the spiritual foundation that she mentored to her children. Like so many mothers, her love and faith outweighed her personal challenges and moments of despair. There was always a sense of prayerfulness that surrounded her as she faced the difficulties of raising children in the Detroit area. I can still hear the words "**PEACE BE STILL**".

Dr. Robert Anthony stated that *"overcoming fear and worry can be accomplished by living a day at a time or even a moment at a time. Your worries will be cut down to nothing".*

When we begin to live our lives one day, one moment at a time, we can manage the many challenges and adversities that come our way. When we take this moment and breath in this spirit of "YES WE CAN" every moment of the day, we will see the shift in our consciousness taking place, moving from that victim's mentality to an attitude of Joshua. Step by step, moment by moment—the way is simple, even if it is not easy.

It has been stated that *"the most authentic thing about us is our capacity to create, to overcome, to endure, to transform, to love and to be greater than our suffering."*

We have to know that this is our day for transformation, moving beyond FEAR, past doubt by putting an end to worry. This attitude cannot just be worthless words of intellect or a faithless sermon on what one might be able to do, or be. The reality is this; we each already have the strength and presence within us to meet every challenge before us.

Nelson Mandela showed us the incredible inner strength of overcoming through the trial and tribulation that he faced in the prison of South Africa. During that time, while he was carrying the faith of a nation on his shoulders, he battled the fear of imprisonment and abuse. He had to reach deep within himself those many lonely nights from the darkness of his prison cell out to a higher spiritual consciousness. His faith, his connection to the presence within, his moment by moment 'peace be still' was able to uplift an entire nation of people upon his release.

"I learned that courage was not the absence of fear, but the triumph over it."

His determination not to allow fear to alter his spiritual vision, internal will, and commitment to world peace and freedom from the injustice and abuses of apartheid demonstrated for the all of us how perfect love overcomes fear.

His message and those of others whose life would not allow the illusion and deception of fear to cripple them from achieving their goal or pursuing their dream is our gift today. We can learn from their sacrifice and inner strength that what they founded was not built on the footsteps of hatred, but on the purity of love.

In this spiraling message of life, our responsibility is to learn that the core of our being is love. It is the first, primary and only force that lives within us as the image and presence of God. When those moments occur where we are challenged by life's issues, we need to remember that we have the internal ability to reach within ourselves to affirm this one and only truth that, "God is my source to meet and to uplift me above any challenge or obstacle that invites fear into my mind, for I know that God is love."

I can never say that one will not encounter those moments in life when fear will present itself, or those moments when we're facing that surging emotion of panic and dreadfulness. In truth, fear will always be with us while we're in this human form. The key becomes our response to fear. When we feel that faithless emotion seeking to invade our consciousness, we need to seek our faithfulness in the assurance that we are God's children, blessed and endowed with a divine spark of life that will not fail us nor desert us.

Don Miguel Ruiz, in his book the "Four Agreements", speaks about a term he calls "Domestication" which describes how we, as spiritual beings, are domesticated or socialized into our society with a set of agreements. One of the methods of domestication is the use of punishment and rewards. We are punished for rules that we don't follow and rewarded for

behaviors that follow the rules.

After a period of being punished or rewarded we cultivate a sense of fear or joy around the expected behaviors. Our mind begins to adapt to this domestication and conditioning, and soon this faithless emotion called fear acts like parasite that weakens our sense of freedom, courage and knowledge of our spiritual self. It creates a broken alignment, a separation with our true self—God.

Our quest is to strengthen this awareness of the process and result of domestication in our consciousness concerning fear and all the negative behavior patterns that it creates. Our quest is to take steps to reclaim our life from fear and to replace it with courage and to begin this self-healing process of alignment with our divine self. We can break these chains by living spiritual principles as taught by our Master Teachers.

Chapter Six

THE HEALING OF FEAR BEGINS IN THE MIND AND BODY

"YOU CAN CONQUER ALMOST ANY FEAR IF YOU WILL MAKE UP YOUR MIND TO DO SO. FOR REMEMBER, FEAR DOESN'T EXIST ANYWHERE EXCEPT IN THE MIND."

DALE CARNEGIE

One of our most difficult challenges in regards to fear is when we face a physical illness. Our mind can plummet into fear when it hears a diagnosis of a dreaded disease or hear the words *no known cure available*.

I have had my own battle with this fear when I was diagnosed with polio as a child. Polio was a crippling disease that left those who had it struggling for their life. I remember it vividly, as if it were yesterday; the smell of the hospital, the gloom of the concerned faces that were around me. My fears were a part of my life that I faced each day.

My mother became my source of relief as she began to teach me, through prayer, how to center my thoughts on the faith of God within me. She taught me to let go of my fears by placing in my mind an affirmation that allowed me to focus on the good in my life:

"For I am one with the universal life forces flowing through my mind and my body bringing me new life and energy, nothing can come to me but good."

Over the years, I was able to change my thoughts from fear to the goodness of God, and my mother's prayers became the internal medicine which began to heal my body and soul.

Each of us at some point in our lives may face a serious health challenge and feel an enormous amount of fear. Those moments will be our testimony to how we view and believe the truth within ourselves; that God is our source and the healing active principle within us. Some of the most inspiring stories come to us from those healing miracles of life that open our hearts and mind to the conscious presence and grace of God.

There was a wonderful friend of mind who spent several years fighting to be released from the parasitical power of fear of open spaces called agoraphobia. She shared with me how she searched for healing support from varies therapies and doctors who failed to find her the relief she needed.

After years of searching, she finally discovered that the path for her healing was within her. She began to open the doors of her spiritual consciousness and sought prayer and meditation as her main therapy and treatment. She surrendered herself to an inner guidance of Truth and began to quietly affirm:

"The light of God surrounds me
The love of God enfold me
The power of God protects me
The presence of God watches over me
Wherever I Am God is."

These words entered into her consciousness with a healing energy that brought peace into life. She felt a calm that she hadn't felt for years. Her fears were still there, but they no longer controlled her thoughts or her body. She used this emotion of fear as a gift to motivate her to achieve her calling in life.

Dianne A. Rhodes shares her story of challenging fear and finding courage. Her story was written for the world to know how perfect love overcomes fear and provides the courage needed for healing and peace in her essay entitled: *The Birth of EVERLASTING*, by Dianne A. Rhodes.

EVERLASTING

My Father's love is everlasting
Steadfast, Strong
It shall not leave me
It does not sway like the sweeping of the tide
Nor does it pale with the passage of my years.
My Father's love is everlasting
Steadfast, Strong
It shall not leave me
What fear have I of the uncertain?
Was it not He by Daniel's side?
My joy
My comfort
My thankful heart at peace
Steadfast, Strong
It shall not leave me
My Father's love is everlasting.

"I had all the Bible verses, inspirational books and prayers from family and friends could provide. What I did not have is faith in the God power within myself. My doctor surmised that I needed surgery and at that moment, I thought I had it all together. Having had four c-sections, I was not a stranger to going under the scalpel. Three of those times I had nine months to prepare and the end results were miracles of life. This time, I didn't have nine months to think about an unscheduled and unplanned surgery.

After the news, I confidently told the surgeon to work me in for another x-ray because I believed God was healing me. He did not budge. "Mrs. Rhodes," he said, "you cannot wait for another gallbladder attack."

How arrogant could a man be—and such prayerlessness! My thoughts went to a strong desire to remind him just where he got his skills from and of who would actually be operating on me, through him. He was just an instrument and I expected him to humble himself and acknowledge that miracles do happen all the time. In fact, I believe miracles are what are to be, all the time. He was in the "supporting God business", not the "I know what is best" business.

Now, I do believe things happen for a reason and we are responsible for the majority of things that happen to us. Water has never been my favorite nourishment (it is now!) and if I had been more conscious of, and responsible for, my unhealthy eating habits and listened to my body, things would be different.

Isn't hindsight wonderful? Lessons learned—no blame just my gain. With much apprehension, I agreed to the surgery. The surgeon had given me hope that if there was not a lot of scar tissue from the c-sections, I could have the mini version or laparoscopic cholecystectomy surgery. That meant that the recovery time would be just about a week. That was worth praying for. If I had to go through this, let it be by the easiest method in the shortest amount of time, with the smallest scar, I could live with that.

So there I was, ready to put added work on my liver by having my gallbladder taken out (thank you, liver) and agreeing to say good-bye to fried foods, chips, fries—you know, all the good stuff—and contemplating a love affair with water. Then, the surgeon tells me about the risks and complications. Here is where the poem comes in. I was scared and all the praying people, inspirational books and truth knowledge did not add up to a hill of lint! That is the point when you can either let go of your faith completely or completely take hold of it. Knowing "The Truth" **will** set you free—but try applying that principle without adding faith when your back is against the wall; it will be evident that just knowing can't match the powerful illusion of **FEAR**!

Everlasting came from taking hold of faith. If I could not take anything physical into the operating room with me (good luck charms, my mother's comforting hand, a crucifix, Star of David or a frog of faith) I was taking God's love over fear and that was enough.

In the end, I had the surgery and it took a year before I felt like I was healed. It is funny how things turn out. I also ended up working for the same surgeon and if you ever go to his office, you will see my framed poem over the desk where he schedules his surgeries. My Father's love *is* everlasting."

Dianne's God-inspired courage gave her the inner strength to conquer the fear of illness and surgery and produced her healing.

There are millions of healing stories that demonstrate the power of Christ, personal stories that express the power of love to overcome fear so that healing can begin. These individuals I honor, for their stories give us continual lessons of hope and healing.

My friend Judy tells her story of miraculous healing in the face of a sudden and disastrous life or death accident.

"Tom, the love of my life and I were walking across a street enjoying the time with each other when, out of nowhere, a light truck struck my beloved 78 year old very healthy husband. He lay on the road convulsing and hemorrhaging from the force of the hit. My initial reaction was total all consuming hysterical fear and rage.

"The paramedics rushed us the nearest community hospital. After a brief assessment at the local hospital in this resort town, most equipped to deal with sunburn and food poisoning, Tom was airlifted to a trauma level 1 hospital in Munson, Michigan, 40 miles away. I had to drive by myself, in the dark, down a two lane winding road in hilly country that I had never driven on before, to find this special hospital I had never been to, on my own, fearful beyond sanity about my barely alive husband.

"During this ride, I knew that I just had to "hang on" and drive through the tears and consuming hysteria. At the trauma hospital, the attending gave me the grim news—severe traumatic brain injury with bleeding in three lobes, multiple skull fractures, significant nerve damage in the skull and a crushed left side of the chest. How do you handle that set of facts?

"But after the trauma specialist left, the PA told me something to give me hope. He said, quite surprised, that Tom's CT scans at Munson's trauma center were actually a little better than the ones we received from the first hospital. He said that was really unheard of.

"It was at that moment I knew that God had a plan and that was all I needed to know. One of the first calls I made after the accident was to our minister Rev. Greg Guice. By the time we got to Munson, I knew that there were people all over the United States praying for Tom.

"When I was told that Tom was improving rapidly it was like God had sent a beam of light for me to hold onto throughout this new chapter in my life. While there were certainly bleak times in the ensuing four and a half months of hospitalization, my fear was overcome with the certainty that God was in charge and he clearly had plans for this wonderful man.

"Tom did his part. He was very compliant despite pain and setbacks throughout the journey. The doctors did their part by utilizing cutting edge treatment, and God did his part by holding us all in his hands and walking with us throughout the journey.

"What overwhelmed me was the power and speed of spreading prayer. My son in Arizona called his pastor immediately. My daughter in Atlanta did the same. Our daughter in Lake Orion called all of her spiritual support groups and asked for prayers. Within days, we had reports of prayers being said for Tom and me throughout the United States, North and South Carolina, Florida, Georgia, California, Denver, Alabama, Oregon Washington. It was amazing. This prayer and circle of spiritual friends enveloped us in love. The beam of light from God sent by these prayers and friends became the source of strength that kept me in faith not fear even today as the healing continues."

When we reflect on our own personal life, there are stories within your own experience of life where fear attached itself to you and challenged the process of healing.

In my freshmen year of college at Kentucky State University, I was informed that my brother had been stricken with cancer. The shock was crippling to me. I didn't want to believe it nor accept it. The greatest challenge occurred when I had to help Haywood (or "Woodie" as we lovingly called him) during his most difficult time.

That summer, while I was at his house, I witnessed the cancer reducing him physically. He lost so much weight that it pained me to look at him as this disease stole the life from a man that served as my mentor, brother and my role model. I was crying inside as the fear of him dying was constantly on my mind.

As the reality set in that these might be the last few days we would share with him, I had to reach somewhere deep within for courage and strength to find the answer to "why him"? This pushed me into realms of unknown territories of thought. I did not have an answer. All I knew was that my brother was dying. Fear became my bedside demon that stalked me in those midnight hours.

I give thanks to my older brothers, Roderic and Johnny, who taught me how to believe in myself and find strength. They shared with me how much "Woodie" loved us and how his love was the strength of our family. Somewhere in this moment of their brotherly counseling and the strength they exhibited as the perfect love for our family, I lost the fear of him dying and was able see him as a gift to all of us. When that special day came of his passing, we celebrated his 'home going'. My brothers and I took a moment to toast his life and give thanks for his perfect love.

Death, for most of us, is the fear of all fears. We live with it constantly wondering whether or not this unknown aspect of life is final or not. I truly believe there is no death. There is only life into life eternal.

Over the years, I've learned to no longer see death as this fearful demon, but as a gift of a passing into a new experience. I have come to learn death as point of growth; my mother's death, and even my daughter's death moved me to a place where I had to embrace this journey of life with perfect love. This greatest fear is always at our doorstep with each turn of life. Jesus' message to us has been to fear no longer for 'I am the way, the truth and the life'.

Unity School of Christianity published a Book of Silent Prayers in 1969 and in that wonderful small book there was a healing prayer for Healing and Renewal to ease the pain of fear.

"Your body is the temple of the living God. God's pure life and substance now renew and rebuild His holy temple."

Emmet Fox in his book "Make Your Life Worth-While" states,

"You can heal any condition if you can get rid of the fear attaching to it. Trouble or sickness is nothing but subconscious fear out pictured in our surroundings. It is true at all times that "we have nothing to fear but fear."

Today we have a great opportunity to show this infinite presence within ourselves and to provide to our children this great demonstration of truth. Together we can reclaim our true self, for we are the instrument of God's presence living out His creation.

"Yea though I walk through the valley and shadow of death I will fear no evil for thou art with me"

For there is a spiritual quality within each of us that enables us to remain poised in a healing knowing that there is no fear, for GOD IS—I AM—that living healing presence in demonstration. GOD IS—I AM.

SEVEN SPIRITUAL KEYS TO OVERCOME FEAR

"AS WE ARE LIBERATED FROM OUR FEARS, OUR PRESENCE AUTOMATICALLY LIBERATES OTHERS."
MARIANNE WILLIAMSON

What is it that gives individuals the ability to overcome their challenges, their inner battles with fear? How can we learn to align with our own greatness and obtain that spirit of victory and liberation?

As I strengthened my connection to God and God's good, as I studied the Bible and the words of Jesus and other great men of spirit, I found key thoughts and affirmations that gave me strength, wisdom, and inner assurance. These I call my Seven Spiritual Keys to conquer fear. I refer to them as Spiritual Keys because they have had the ability to unlock the door to that mighty Presence within where courage and healing grace appear to me in my time of need. I have found that they are universal spiritual truisms and they can act as tools to conquer FEAR.

These spiritual keys, when taken in, spoken, repeated, prayed over and meditated upon, can and will produce a steady *knowingness* of assurance that feeds our spiritual cells. They become foundational pillars in our consciousness that affirms an inner truth and aligns our Christ consciousness with our heart and our mind so when we face our fears, we can draw from this inner *knowingness* the courage that we will need to overcome adversity.

You will find that each key begins with the word *"know"*. In this time of our world, we must begin to activate a sense of knowingness that aligns us with the universe and that Christ presence within. There is no room for "IF" or "MAYBE". The universe is created through the energy of I AM. We must operate with the attitude and awareness of affirming the assurance of God's presence within us; I KNOW that GOD IS, and I AM.

It is our responsibility to integrate our spiritual awareness into our life, not as an intellectual discourse, but as a daily practice of thought. Our spiritual design is capable to overcome the challenges before us; the key is in our connection to the oneness of God.

The First Spiritual Key:

"KNOW THAT GOD IS YOUR SOURCE TO OVER-COME ALL ADVERSITY"

When you **know** God as your source, there is a powerful certainty that you are able to draw from within yourself and it provides the strength and courage needed to overcome any adversity, any fear.

This spiritual key embodies **Faith** that becomes like a backbone in times of trouble. Knowing God as your source of all supply including courage is an essential ingredient for facing all fears.

Take a moment and reflect on the importance of this spiritual key. Our ability to **know** God as this inner source of power and protection can create a Joshua-like courage to face our giants, one by one and see they are nothing.

The question may arise, how do I know and how do I begin to acquire this knowingness that God is my source?

You arrive at that answer by simply becoming still and taking a moment and affirming these words:

"God is the infinite presence of good and the only source within me."

The Second Spiritual Key:

"KNOW AND AFFIRM BEFORE ANY CHALLENGE THAT "I CAN DO ALL THINGS THROUGH CHRIST WHICH STRENGTHENS ME."

Our fears and challenges can be like immovable mountains; so big, so high, so real that we shrink into our small personal self feeling helpless. We can't see the answer to our problems. But God asks us to lean on Him, for 'He doeth the works." As we affirm with our mind and our heart that we can do all things through that anointed presence, we create within ourselves a surge of energy that pours forth to give us the strength that one will need to meet any challenge.

Close your eyes and feel this energy flowing through out your body, and declare that *"I can do all things through Christ which strengthens me"*. These words will become crystallized within you and your heart beat will find a rhythm of peace and calm. There will flow out from you a confidence and a knowingness that meets each challenge with an attitude of "Yes I Can".

Let go of any fear or doubt and know that right now God is with you. Breathe in this awareness and see yourself moving through this moment as you affirm . . .

"I CAN DO ALL THINGS THROUGH CHRIST WHICH STRENGTHENS ME"

The Third Spiritual Key:

"KNOW AND AFFIRM THAT "GOD IS MY ROCK AND MY FOUNDATION, I SHALL NOT YIELD."

When facing a difficult situation, become still and know that God as your foundation will not allow you to fail. Do not yield to the appearance of a difficult moment. In every situation affirm the omnipotent power of God as that foundational energy which abides within you dissolving any fear and casting out all doubt. Say, in those moments of despair or adversity, I shall not yield for "God is my, rock and my foundation".

When we know the power of God as the only and highest functioning presence within us, it will bring poise to the mind and our faith will become as solid as a rock.

Quiet your mind right now and feel God's presence flowing within every cell, every muscle, and with every thought. Know that God's presence brings a peace of mind to your consciousness. This unmovable belief becomes the foundation of *knowing* that the Kingdom of God is within you. It is your inner sanctuary of faith and upon this rock you will be able to stand before any obstacle and say "I Shall Not yield".

"THE LORD IS MY ROCK AND MY FORTRESS AND MY DELIVERER, MY GOD, MY STRENGTH, IN WHOM I WILL TRUST."

The Fourth Spiritual Key:

"KNOW THAT WHENEVER THE STORMS OF FEAR ARISE WITHIN YOU, BECOME STILL AND AFFIRM THAT THE "THE LORD IS MY LIGHT AND MY SALVATION, AND I SHALL NOT FEAR, PEACE BE STILL."

In the very moment when you feel a surging energy of fear paralyzing every movement in your body and you feel this uncontrollable raging emotion of lack or doubt pouring into your mind, become still and breathe into your consciousness that affirming thought "the Lord is my Light and my Salvation". Remember that light is the "understanding principle in mind". It is a symbol of wisdom and Truth.

Salvation comes to us as a gift when we are in oneness with the awareness of God's ability to quiet any storm, to bring peace to any situation, and to instill that calm spirit.

This Spiritual Key calms the mind of worry, doubt, or fear. Take this moment and see those raging storms becoming a gentle breeze of truth flowing in your life as you echo the words "Peace Be Still".

"MY HEART IS AT PEACE, FOR I KNOW THAT GOD IN HIS LOVE HAS SET ME FREE FROM FEAR, I AM ASSURED OF HIS CONSTANT BLESSING AND I AM UNAFRAID."

The Fifth Spiritual Key:

"KNOW THAT WITH PRAYER AND MEDITATION, I AM STRENGTHENING EACH DAY WITH AN UNYIELDING COURAGE TO SEE THE OUTPOURING OF GOOD IN ALL SITUATIONS AND IN ALL THINGS."

Prayer and meditation become the harmonizing force that aligns our consciousness with our divinity. Prayer becomes this highly accelerated mind action that expresses God's will. Meditation expands our Christ consciousness and brings into our realization that there is within us this unyielding courage to overcome all things and to see the good in each moment of life.

When we pray, our hearts become open to God's will, knowing that it is God's good pleasure to give us the kingdom. Prayer is a communion between God and man. It brings to our consciousness the oneness with God.

With prayer we strengthen ourselves in harmony with the universe as we see only the good in all of our affairs. Yes, even in the face of adversity, look for the good or pray to be shown the good. Many times we find that out of adversity, a new life emerges better than before and we rejoice in these blessings!

Let us become still in this moment and know that every thought is a prayer. Breathe in the awareness that God Is, I AM. Do not dwell on any other thought but truth. Just let go and experience the stillness of Christ, and know these words, there is no fear in Christ.

"PRAYER AND MEDITATION QUIET OUR MIND AND SET US FREE FROM OUR DOUBT, WORRY AND LIMITATIONS."

The Sixth Spiritual Key:

"KNOW AND DECLARE THAT "GOD HAS NOT GIVEN ME A SPIRIT OF FEAR, BUT OF POWER AND LOVE AND A SOUND MIND."

There is a knowingness that must be declared within one's being, that "our Father which art in heaven" has not given us a spirit of fear, doubt, nor worry. We are filled with the power of love, and perfect love casts out all fear.

This spiritual key describes an active moving force within us, a vibration, a spiritual principle that instills a truth within our being that becomes operative when we declare that "God has not given me a spirit of fear, but of power and love and a sound mind."

Make this declaration, "God has not given me a spirit of fear". As you say these words, the very cells within your being become an active principle of life and take on the character and nature of the declaration.

The awareness that God has not given you a spirit of fear strengthens that moment with courage and power and your mind draws into its consciousness a Christ love that erases any disharmony within the mind and body caused by this false emotion created through worry, doubt, or fear.

"GOD'S PERFECT LOVE POURS INTO MY BEING CASTING OUT ALL FEAR AND DECLARING THAT GOD IS MY SOURCE AND STRENGTH."

The Seventh Spiritual Key:

KNOW AND AFFIRM:

"I AM A CONQUER THROUGH THE REALIZATION THAT THERE IS ONLY ONE PRESENCE AND ONE POWER ACTIVE IN MY LIFE GOD THE GOOD OMNIPOTENT."

Once you realize that there is only one presence and the anointing power of Christ flowing within you, a divine connection takes place between you and God, a sense of oneness enters into your mind and body. You feel reborn with love and zeal, your life is filled with courage no fear can overcome you.

Close your eyes, and know each letter, each word, as the truth. Let each word vibrate into your consciousness. Then breath them into your being, seeing each cell and every fiber of who you are saying yes to this agreement.

"THERE IS ONLY ONE PRESENCE AND ONE POWER ACTIVE IN MY LIFE GOD THE GOOD OMNIPOTENT."

These spiritual keys are the tools that will help us align with our truth as we face our fears, our adversity or our challenges in life. These spiritual keys are not effective if we don't practice affirming and declaring their truth. They must become a focus of our daily meditation, a central part of a verbal diet for us. As we embrace the keys of *knowing* that we can choose love over fear, strength over weakness, and courage over defeat, we have the tools to conquer fear!

These spiritual keys will develop our faith and will bind within our consciousness the knowledge and Spiritual awareness that we can do all things through Christ.

Charles Fillmore states

"The understanding of Spirit clarifies my faith. My faith is of God and in God. My faith grows greater each day, because it is planted in Truth, and through it the mountains of mortal error are moved into the sea of nothingness. My doubts and fears are dissolved and dissipated; in confidence and peace I rest in God's unchangeable Law. My faith comprehends the beauty of wholeness. I am persuaded that God is

able, that He is willing, and that He is eager to give me whatsoever I ask."

In the final analysis our ability to conquer fear can be as simple as our reflection on our child like ability to remember who and what we are, **"CHILDREN OF GOD"**.

The Final Thoughts

I leave you with a final story, another song from my youth.

It occurred the last year that I was in middle school, the year was 1967. During those moments in Detroit my life was filled with difficulties. I had to always search for courage to overcome my fears which seem to stalk me on every corner.

One summer day, while walking home from my little league baseball game, not paying attention to the smell of smoke in the air, or the continuous sound of fire trucks racing up and down the streets, I found myself in the mist of an urban storm; the infamous riots of Detroit were underway. The streets were ablaze with people looting and shouting their frustration over the racism and injustice which had become a sad story within America.

These nights for me became moments of petrifying fear as I watched police wrestle with people day and night. I saw National Guard troops driving jeeps through the neighborhood. You could hear their gun fire each night.

The street became a battle zone that carried with it the heartfelt sound of fear. My fear reached its peak one night when I was at home. Out of nowhere the sound of gunfire was heard outside of our house. My mother quickly instructed us to get on the floor. That gunfire continued for what felt to us like a life time.

When it finally came to an end, I could still feel my heart racing and pounding well into the night. My mother determined that it was safe to send us to bed, and as she comforted us, she prayed with us. She put on some James Cleveland and Motown songs to sooths all of us.

There was one song that I never forgot. It was a song by Stevie Wonder called "With a Child's Heart". That song comforted me as I think back. I believe the words from that song allowed me to go to a center of peace and comfort.

The words stay in mind to this very day as words of comfort and peace in moments of fear . . .

"With a child's heart
Go face the worries of the day
With a child's heart
Turn each problem into play
No need to worry no need to fear
Just being alive makes it all so very clear
With a child's heart
Nothing can ever get you down
With a child's heart
You've got no reason to frown
Love is as welcome
As a sunny sunny day
No grown up thoughts
To lead our hearts astray
Take life easy, so easy nice and easy
Like a child so gay and so carefree
The whole world smiles with you
As you go your merry way
Oh with a child's heart
Nothing's gonna get you down

If there was a message that Jesus instilled within us it's the message that we must become as little children, open to the presence of the Christ within. For there in that sacred center of truth we embrace this perfect love which overcomes this False Emotion Acting Real; FEAR.

When we know divine love as that child's quality of spirit, we can be fearless and selfless in that perfect state of being and Truth. To be in that Christ consciousness filled with the quietness and confidence of Jesus, to practice the presence of this divine Truth is to know no fear for "I AM WITH THEE".

The greatest joy for me comes in knowing that the presence of God lives within. In writing this book I had to look deep within myself and become both the subject and the observer. What I learned from the many personal stories and memories shared, is that we do not have to allow fear to dominate our thoughts and mind. We do have within us the power to overcome and to conquer fear when we realize our true nature. Jesus Christ taught us that we are more than conqueror we are children of God.

GOD IS, I AM !

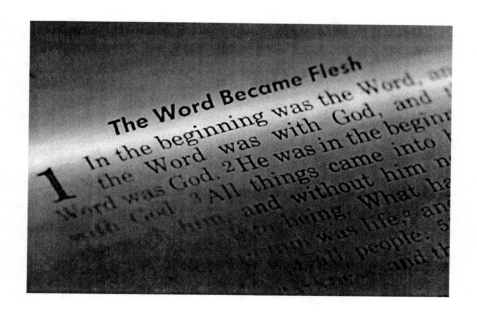

Inspirational Quotes For The Courage To Conquer FEAR

"We must build dikes of courage to hold back the flood of fear."

(Martin Luther King Jr.)

"We have chosen hope over fear."

(*Barack Obama*)

"Stand up to your obstacles and do something about them. You will find that they haven't half the strength you think they have."

(*Norman Vincent Peale*)

"If you want to conquer fear, do not sit home and think about it. Go out and get busy."

(*Dale Carnegie*)

"I feel that the most important requirement in success is learning to overcome failure. You must learn to tolerate it, but never accept it."

(**Reggie Jackson**)

"The only thing we have to fear is fear itself."

(**Franklin D. Roosevelt**)

"Decide that you want it more than you are afraid of it."

(**Bill Cosby**)

"Search for the seed of good in every adversity."

(**Og Mandino**)

"Rise above the storm and you will find the sunshine."

(**Mario Fernandez**)

"Success is not measured by the heights one attains, but by the obstacles one overcome in its attainment."

(**Booker T. Washington**)

"I count him braver who overcomes his desire than him who conquest his; for the hardest victory is over self."

(**Aristotle**)

"The greater the obstacle, the more the glory in overcoming it."

(**Jean Baptiste Moliere**)

"Few will have the greatness to bend history itself, but each of us can work to change a small portion of events . . . It is from numberless acts of courage and belief that human history is shaped."

(**John F. Kennedy**)

"Courage comes by taking action before you are forced to."

(Iyanla Vanzant)

"I learned that courage was not the absence of fear, but the triumph over it. The brave man is not he who does not feel, but he who conquers that fear."

(Nelson Mandela)

"Nothing in life is to be feared, It is only to be understood."

(Marie Curie)

"Fear is a disease that eats away at logic and makes man inhuman."

(Marian Anderson)

"Courage is not the lack of fear it is acting in spite of it."

(Mark Twain)

"You gain strength, courage, and confidence by every experience in which you really stop to look fear in the face. You must do the right thing which you think you cannot do."

(Eleanor Roosevelt)

"When our days become dreary with low hovering clouds of despair, and when our nights become darker than midnights, let us remember that there is a creative force in this universe, working to pull down the gigantic mountains of evils, a power that is able to make a way out of no way and transform dark yesterdays into bright tomorrows. Let us realize the arc of the moral universe is long but it bends toward justice."

(Martin Luther King Jr.)

"Our deepest fear is not that we are inadequate. Our deepest fear is that we are powerful beyond measure. It is our light not our darkness that frightens us. We ask ourselves who am I to be brilliant, gorgeous, talented and fabulous? Actually who are you not to be? You are a child of God. Your playing small doesn't serve the world. There's nothing enlightened about shrinking so that other people won't feel insecure around you. We were born to make manifest the glory of God that is within us. It is not just in some of us; it's in everyone. And as we let our light shine, we unconsciously give other people permission to do the same. As we are liberated from our fear, our presence automatically liberates others."

(Marianne Williamson)

"Opposition is a natural part of life. Just as we develop our physical muscles through overcoming opposition—such as weights—we develop our character muscles by overcoming challenges and adversity"

(Stephen R. Covey)

"Obstacles can't stop you. Problems can't stop you. Most of all people can't stop you. Only you can stop you."

(Jeffery Gitomer)

"Learning to overcome fear in its insidious manifestations is to learn the power and manifestation of faith."

(Johnnie Jones)

"He who fears of being conquered is sure of defeat"

(Napoleon Bonaparte)

"Fear is met and destroyed with courage"

(James F. Bell)

"No passion so effectually robs the mind of its powers of acting and reasoning as fear."

(Edmund Burke)

"Failure is success if we learn from it"

(Mario Andretti)

"Do not fear the winds of adversity. Remember: A kite rises against the wind rather than with it."

(Author Unknown)

"I know God will not give me anything I can't handle. I just wish that He didn't trust me so much."

(Mother Teresa)

"Every adversity, every failure, every heartache carries with it the seed of an equal or greater benefit."

(Napoleon Hill)

"Every problem has in it the seeds of its own solution. If you don't have any problems, you don't get any seeds."

(Norman Vincent Peale)

"The first duty of man is to conquer fear; he must get rid of it, he cannot act till then."

(Thomas Carlyle)

"Too many of us are not living our dreams because we are living our fears."

(Les Brown)

"Comfort your fears, list them, get to know them, and only then will you be able to put them aside and move ahead."

(Jerry Gillies)

LaVergne, TN USA
03 April 2011
222699LV00008B/224/P